A selection of carved and painted wares from Poole's Delphis range, 1960s.

Ceramics of
the 1960s

Graham McLaren

A Shire book

Published in 2001 by Shire Publications Ltd, Cromwell
House, Church Street, Princes Risborough,
Buckinghamshire HP27 9AA, UK.
(Website: www.shirebooks.co.uk)

British Library Cataloguing in Publication Data:
McLaren, Graham
Ceramics of the 1960s. – (A Shire book)
1. Ceramics – History – 20th century 2. Ceramic industries
– Great Britain – History – 20th century
I. Title 738'.0941'09046
ISBN 0 7478 0486 9

Front cover: *A range of ceramics from the 1960s: (from left to right) Impact vase,
Stylised Cat, Home Décor vase (all Hornsea); dish in blue Totem (front), coffee pot in
Gold Phoenix (rear) (both Portmeirion); Delphis plant pot (Poole).*
Back cover: *Studio cup and saucer in a shape developed by the studio potter Kenneth
Clark, with decoration designed by Glyn Colledge, Denby, 1961.*

ACKNOWLEDGEMENTS
Many people have been of assistance in the production of this book. In particular I would
like to thank the following: Tom Arnold, Ruth Brown, Miranda Goodby, David Puxley,
Alan Rogers, Brian Sullivan, Alan Swale, Wendy Wort, the owners and staff of the Ginnel
Gallery, the Local Studies Librarian at Keele University.
Photographs are acknowledged as follows: author's collection, back cover, pages 5 (top), 7
(top left and right), 8 (bottom left and right), 11 (bottom left), 12, 13 (top), 16 (above right and
bottom), 18 (top), 19 (bottom), 21 (centre left and bottom), 22 (bottom right), 23 (top), 25
(bottom), 27 (bottom left and right), 28 (centre and bottom), 31 (bottom left), 34 (bottom), 36
(bottom); Tom Arnold, pages 33 (top), 40; Richard Dennis Publications, pages 1, 3, 25 (top
and centre); the Ginnel Gallery, pages 6, 9 (both), 10 (bottom), 17 (top right), 19 (top left and
right centre), 22 (centre), 24 (bottom), 29 (bottom), 30 (bottom), 32 (top), 35 (centre and top
right), 36 (top), 37 (top); Keele University Local Studies Collection, pages 4 (bottom), 16
(above left), 23 (bottom right), 24 (top), 26 (both), 27 (top right), 29 (top), 37 (bottom), 38
(top); Mrs Joan McLaren, page 5 (bottom); Portmeirion Potteries Ltd, page 18 (bottom); the
Potteries Museum and Art Gallery, pages 21 (top and centre right), 22 (top), 23 (centre), 30
(top), 31 (top and bottom right), 38 (bottom); David Puxley, pages 13 (bottom), 14 (top), 39;
Alan Rogers, pages 7 (bottom), 20; Staffordshire University, pages 10 (top), 15 (centre), 32
(bottom); Brian Sullivan (email:artbas@staffs.ac.uk), pages 4 (top), 11 (top and centre), 14
(bottom), 15 (top), 17 (left), 28 (top); Alan Swale, pages 8 (top), 33 (bottom).

Printed in Malta by Gutenberg Press Ltd, Gudja Road,
Tarxien PLA 19, Malta.

Contents

White earthenware Poole Atlantis studio vase, 1960s.

A colourful decade

Above: *Anemone, hand-painted oven-to-table ware by the Finnish firm of Arabia, late 1960s.*

The 1960s were particularly successful years for British art and design. Britain finally emerged from the long shadows cast by the Second World War and re-established herself as an international force in visual culture. Names such as Mary Quant, Twiggy and the Beatles may be clichés now, but they indicate the significance of the decade.

The design of ceramics of the 1960s reflects the dynamism of the period. During the 1950s ceramic design was dominated by a reaction to the austerity of war and British manufacturers had looked to designs from countries like Italy and Sweden for a modern design aesthetic. Although these influences undoubtedly continued, most of the stylistic roots for ceramic design of the 1960s were British.

Pottery manufacturers in the 1960s mastered the decorative techniques of photo-lithography and screen printing first introduced during the early post-war years. Contemporary art movements such as Pop used the look and the processes of commercial design. Ceramic designers in turn used the bright, opaque colours created by screen printing to imitate the imagery of Pop art.

Burleigh
present....

ORBIT

Fresh and scintillating as if from outer space!

This thrilling new idea in modern tableware is a bold exercise in spatial relationships. It combines a varying degree of depth from the startling whiteness of the body through to the carefully planned colour variations of the motif.

An attractive pattern with a difference!

ORBIT in two exciting colour schemes.

BURGESS & LEIGH LIMITED
MIDDLEPORT POTTERY, BURSLEM
STAFFORDSHIRE ST6 3PE, ENGLAND
London Agent & Showrooms: A. H. N. Glew
6 Holborn Viaduct, London, E.C.1

Left: *Advertised as 'Fresh and scintilating as if from outer space!', Orbit by Burgess & Leigh (c.1969) utilised the imagery of op art to dramatic effect.*

Variation, designed by the famous Finnish designer Tapio Wirkkala and manufactured by the German firm of Rosenthal from 1962, was to have a significant impact on tableware design across Europe with its severe, straight-sided shape.

The 1960s were also a challenging period for the pottery industry with the break-up of the family-owned network of manufacturers that had underpinned it since the Industrial Revolution. Amalgamations were formed, resulting in large con-glomerates that were often divisions of commercial enterprises with little direct interest in ceramic design and manufacture. This was a process that quickly gathered pace and lasted for the rest of the century.

Nineteenth-century and other revivals

In the early years of the 1960s ceramic design was split between a continuing interest in modern continental influences and a revival of earlier styles. A dependence upon past styles had characterised the output of the industry for much of the twentieth century. The Victorian revivals of the 1960s reflect new pressures upon the pottery industry to integrate its designs with other areas of the decorative arts, such as furniture and textiles. Collecting antiques and bric-à-brac became popular pastimes

Tea set in Old Country Roses pattern on Montrose shape by T. C. Wild & Son (Royal Albert) in bone china. Introduced 1962.

and it was considered 'chic' to display an understanding of historical styles, even amongst the young. In ceramics these trends were demonstrated by the tremendous commercial success of the Old Country Roses pattern of T. C. Wild & Son (who operated under the trade name of Royal Albert).

Conceived during the last years of the 1950s and first marketed in 1962, OCR (as the trade came to know it) became one of the most successful patterns to emerge from the industry. It continued to be a worldwide best-seller for the remainder of the twentieth century. The design reflected the new structures and relationships within the industry and was the result of a creative collaboration between T. C. Wild and Capper Rataud Ltd, one of the 'litho houses' that had a significant impact on post-war pattern design. The rich colours of the pattern juxtaposed with gilding on the Montrose shape represented a successful use of photo-lithographic technology and allowed a decorative item to be produced flexibly and economically.

The marketing of OCR reflects the sophistication required to attract the fickle consumers of the day. From its introduction the pattern was sold as single items as well as sets and was aimed at young, aspiring consumers who wished to collect the pattern gradually. Sales were further supported by a sustained marketing campaign combining advertising in women's magazines with television promotion.

The popularity of the Victorian style also offered manufacturers the opportunity to revisit their existing pattern collections. There was an expansion in the number of blue and white patterns available and of adaptations of engravings of the late eighteenth and early nineteenth centuries for contemporary needs.

Portmeirion Thomas Bewick storage jars, 1960s.

Above left: *Posy vases in Floral shape by Hornsea, 1962.*

Above right: *Baroque, by Burgess & Leigh, 1969.*

Another powerful trend was an interest in the style of the late-nineteenth-century Art Nouveau movement, characterised by sinuous, flowing lines. The interest was fuelled by a series of popular exhibitions and discussions in publications. The 1960s version proved as eclectic in its use of historical motifs as that of the original movement. There were references to Art Nouveau's fascination with stylised biological form, as in Hornsea's Floral (1962), manufactured for just one year. Generally, however, the revival was typified by ever more extravagant stylisation of form and vivid colour. By the late 1960s, with examples such as Burgess & Leigh's Baroque (1969), we see the beginnings of a tendency that, boosted by movements such as Op art, emerged into full-blown Psychedelia during the early 1970s.

The Art Nouveau revival was mainly transmitted through surface pattern techniques such as screen printing and photo-lithography. This helps to explain how new shapes such as Midwinter's Fine (see page 10) and J. & G. Meakin's Studio survived the twists and turns of 1960s fashion as carriers of these patterns.

One of the most interesting branches of the revival featured motifs from Dark Age and Christian Celtic cultures and continued through the second half of the decade. It encompassed surface pattern, such as Empire Porcelain's lithographic

Bali on Studio shape by Alan Rogers for J. & G. Meakin, 1969. The pattern was intended to '... share the richness of Javanese art'.

7

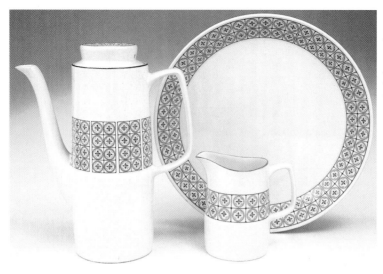

Iona on Image 70 shape, both designed by Alan Swale for Empire Porcelain, 1964.

Iona on its Image 70 shape (1964) by Alan Swale, and types where the motifs were part of the shape itself. Of these, examples like Saxony by the Ellgreave Pottery (in production 1968) also show the popularity of oven-to-table ware.

Another good example is provided by Crown Clarence's Agincourt (1968), designed by David Metcalfe and Diane Ingleheart. The company tended to follow rather than lead fashion, but Agincourt represented a significant investment backed by trade advertising emphasising that '... great attention

has been paid to the mode of living of the younger generation'. The bullish approach taken by the designers drawing on British design heritage is typical of the late 1960s. In the words of *The Pottery Gazette*, 'They wanted a truly British feeling, and in

Above: *Saxony oven-to-table ware casserole utilising Celtic motifs, 1968.*

Right: *Cup and saucer in Agincourt pattern by Crown Clarence, 1968. Described as '... a sophisticated version of medieval and Tudor pottery', it was immediately accepted for the Design Index.*

Coffee pot and cup and saucer in Sienna pattern by Jessie Tait on Fine shape, W. R. Midwinter, 1962.

looking at all that British potters had produced in the past, eschewed influences which had come from abroad through the various ages.'

British Modern style

The contrast between this historical revivalism and 'contemporary' design seems stark. Late 1950s examples such as Royal College by Spode (1959) were influenced by the organic qualities of the Scandinavian form of modern design. This resulted in rounded, curvaceous shapes deemed suitable for conservative British tastes and capable of carrying traditional as well as contemporary patterns.

By the early 1960s modern ceramic design in Britain seemed to be adopting a much sparer, more rigorous approach. The soft shapes of the late 1950s gave way to designs based on cylindrical and tubular forms. The most significant early example of this

A range of patterns on Fine shape. Left to right: Graphic, Oakley, Queensberry. W. R. Midwinter, 1960s.

9

Tankard in cream-coloured earthenware with decoration of black enamel stripes. Staffordshire, c.1770. David Queensberry emphasised the links between traditional eighteenth-century British designs like this and his Fine shape for Midwinter.

trend is David Queensberry's Fine shape for Midwinter, introduced in 1962. Queensberry had been appointed professor of ceramics at the Royal College of Art in London in 1959 and emphasised modernity and flexibility in design rather than allegiance to the historical traditions of the industry. He had already made his reputation working for firms like Crown Staffordshire, where he developed modern shapes in porcelain. The austere quality of Fine suggests a move towards continental forms, and particularly German modernity. In discussing the shape, however, Queensberry emphasised the formal links he had made with the creamware traditions of eighteenth-century Staffordshire and the inspiration provided by the peculiarly British shape of the milk churn. Although Fine avoids obvious historical revivalism, the emphasis on a British derivation for the shape signals a turning away from the wholehearted assimilation of continental prototypes, a trend identified by commentators as British Modern.

The cultural dynamism of 1960s Britain, with Carnaby Street and the King's Road in London emerging as international fashion centres, had youth culture at its heart. The fashion designer Mary Quant in 1962 coined the phrase 'The Look' to refer to the new style. Britain came to be regarded as a world leader in art and design. Added to this was the expected British entry into the European Common Market. Although this was not realised until

Coffee pots in the MQ1 shape, a development of Fine shape by W. R. Midwinter, 1960s. Left to right: Madeira, Lakeland, Country Garden.

the 1970s, many pottery manufacturers saw the need for a recognisably British ceramic style as a defence against continental competition. Fine was an early example of the severe geometric forms that represented The Look in ceramic design. It proved flexible as a vehicle for surface pattern and survived as a commercially successful shape through the decade (the shape was remodelled in 1966 and given the name MQ1).

The geometric form was taken to an extreme by the Cylinder range introduced by Susan Williams-Ellis at Portmeirion from

Above: *Coffee pots and cup and saucer in Totem pattern on Cylinder shape. Portmeirion, 1963.*

Right: *Pieces from a tea set in the unusual white version of Totem. Portmeirion, 1960s.*

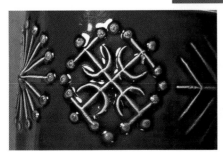

Left: *Detail of a blue-glazed Totem piece showing the exposure of the highest parts of the decorative detail.*

Pieces from a variety of manufacturers that follow the trend started by Portmeirion's Totem pattern, 1960s.

1962 onwards. These slim, attenuated shapes proved adaptable and were covered in a range of glaze types. Totem, introduced in 1963, was a startling early example. This combined stylised motifs loosely based on the heritage of the Native American peoples with glazes that complemented the decorative detail. The nature of the glaze was such that it exposed the highest parts of the decorative motifs in an attractive way. The design sold very well and a wide range of similar pieces from other manufacturers in Britain and abroad attempted to mirror its success.

The popularity of Totem highlights the pressures felt by organisations like the Council of Industrial Design (COID). It believed in a modernist approach to design, emphasising principles such as 'utility' and 'truth to materials'. The slender shape of Totem was of questionable practicality, but in it Williams-Ellis was acknowledging changes in the design process and a new consumerism based on a fashion cycle in ceramics as in other areas of the decorative arts. The new approach to design recognised the dominance and spending power of the consumer. It also recognised that consumers valued designs like Totem not so much for their practicality as for their role as purely decorative objects with a limited 'life' determined by fashion. Manufacturers struggled to understand these trends. The obsession in the trade press with fashion and with American theories of artificial or planned obsolescence based around a fashion cycle meant that the concerns of the COID were further marginalised.

An illustration from 'Design', May 1960, which demonstrates the type of spare, utilitarian tableware of which the Council of Industrial Design approved. Designed by Axel Bruel for Porcelaens Fabriken 'Danmark' AS, Denmark, early 1960s.

Contrasted with designs like Totem, pieces chosen by the COID for the Design Index and the Design Centre labelling scheme seem dull and limited. The tone in the COID's journal *Design* was generally disapproving when discussing the British design revolution whilst foreign journals were enthusiastically extolling the phenomenon.

Craft values

It is ironic that the COID, established to support and improve the standards of industrial design, preferred the work of British craftspeople. *Design* devoted an article (1965) to the work of potters like Kenneth Clark, Ann Wynn Reeves and Alan Wallwork in tile design. But it was where craft and industrial design could be integrated that the greatest benefit was identified. There are few cases of craftspeople working with industry during the 1960s – David Puxley's work for Wedgwood is one example – but they were most successful in factories where craft values were supported.

Denby, employing studio potters like Glyn Colledge from the 1940s, is particularly significant here. The Chevron range,

Turned vases in basalt stoneware by David Puxley for Wedgwood, early 1960s.

Lamp base with applied decoration and two vases by David Puxley for Wedgwood, early 1960s.

designed by Gillian Pemberton and introduced in 1962, was both a commercial success and an example of this integrated approach to design. Made in stoneware (a body type popularly associated with craft ceramics), the range was decorated by hand with a circular tool called a roulette that impressed the chevron pattern into the surface of the unfired clay. It was, however, the integration of a craft technique with industrial manufacture that made Chevron exciting to the COID.

The integration of the design and manufacturing processes had always been an aspect of modernist thinking. The COID's preference can also be seen as part of a general interest in craft values that represented a rejection of The Look from the middle

Chevron, designed by Gillian Pemberton in stoneware for Denby, 1962.

14

Left: *Detail of Chevron showing the decorative effect created by the action of the roulette on the surface of the wet clay.*

Right: *Bowl, stoneware, with a simple pattern of plant motifs in brown on a buff flecked background. Bernard Leach, 1965–70.*

of the 1960s onwards. These values were epitomised by the work and teachings of the studio potter Bernard Leach, who saw the crafts as a basis for a way of life.

Links can be made between the interest in craft values and the movement of the population away from the industrial towns and cities that continued for the rest of the century. The pottery industry capitalised upon this mood with designs capturing the qualities of craft ceramics whilst retaining the economies of mass manufacture. For example, to advertise its Studio range of oven-to-table ware on a shape originally designed by the studio potter Kenneth Clark, Denby chose to make references to '... grey "hare's fur" glaze'. Industrial manufacturers were mainly content, however, to emphasise certain qualities of craft products such as textured surfaces.

Surface texture was a feature that continued to the end of the decade, taking many different forms. These ranged from very literal interpretations, such as Lord Nelson Pottery's Langdale (1970), intended to '... capture the rugged splendour of the mountainous Lake District from where it takes its name', to serious interpretations of craft values, such as Poole's highly successful Delphis range.

The interest in the countryside also helps explain the popularity of revivalist styles. *The Pottery Gazette* (1965) commented that Royal Albert's Old Country Roses '... fits aptly with the

Above: *Delphis plant pot with incised decoration. Poole, c.1968.*

Left: *Advertisement for Lord Nelson Pottery's Langdale range, 1970.*

Left: *Cup and saucer in Rustic oven-to-table ware by Shorter & Son, 1966. This was described by the trade press as '... peasant style, but produced by the craft of the modern potter'.*

"cottagey" styles which so many customers seek'. 'Peasant style' had fascinated the Western world since the early part of the century; but the rash of new examples appearing during the mid to late 1960s, such as Shorter's Rustic (1966), represents a re-invigoration of this interest.

Above: *Storage jar in Talisman pattern by Portmeirion, 1962. The bold design took advantage of the aesthetic qualities provided by the screen-print process and was also intended for easy and economical application.*

Left: *Part coffee set in Greek Key pattern by Portmeirion, 1965.*

—The principal manufacturers—

Design innovation within the Staffordshire Potteries region during the 1960s was epitomised by **Portmeirion**. The company was founded by Susan Williams-Ellis (daughter of Sir Clough Williams-Ellis, founder and architect of the holiday village of Portmeirion in Wales) and her husband, Euan Cooper-Willis. It was created from an amalgamation of A. E. Gray (bought in January 1960) and Kirkham's Ltd (bought 1961), with the company trading as Portmeirion from January 1962.

This amalgamation proved auspicious. Gray's had built a reputation for good modern decorative design during the inter-war period, whilst Kirkham's were known for utility wares, including basins, pestles and mortars, and apothecary jars. Williams-Ellis, as chief designer for the company throughout the decade, mirrored this coupling in her approach to design, which can be summed up as the innovative linking of bright modern shapes and patterns with a judicious use of historical references.

Portmeirion was helped in this by the discovery of copper-plate engravings and moulds in the attics of Kirkham's, many dating back to the nineteenth century. These were adapted for production to meet the demand for Victorian-style pieces. The most significant legacy of Kirkham's production was a type of technical ceramics called a Porous Cell, its tubular shape acting as the basis for the Cylinder range that dominated the Portmeirion 'look' during the 1960s. Despite its seeming impracticality, Cylinder proved adaptable and remained a viable shape throughout the

17

decade, acting as the basis for patterns such as Talisman (1962), Greek Key (1965), and Gold Phoenix (1968) by assistant designer John Cuffley.

These innovative shapes should not obscure the imaginative approach to pattern design taken by Portmeirion. Early patterns like Malachite (1960) indicate an interest in rich, boldly coloured decoration that drew as much from textile design as from ceramics. Later shapes, still emphasising the cylinder theme, also harmonised with ever more ambitious patterns. The Serif shape (introduced 1963) is an example of this with a less attenuated

body than Totem and a decorative handle that gave the shape its name. Serif acted as the vehicle for patterns such as Gold Rule (1968) and the very successful Magic City (1966), as well as ranges like Cypher and the short-lived Jupiter (both 1963) where decoration was integrated into the body.

Midwinter's output was rather more focused on consolidation. The company had built up an international reputation for thoughtful, innovative design during the 1950s. The company's products gradually changed in the early 1960s. Many earlier patterns survived into the new decade via the continuing success of the Fashion

Above: *Part coffee set in Gold Phoenix pattern by Portmeirion, 1968.*

Right: *Malachite pattern by Portmeirion, 1960. This was an adaptation of an earlier textile pattern by Susan Williams-Ellis but remained in production for only a relatively short period owing to high production costs.*

Above left: *Part coffee set in Magic City by Portmeirion, 1966.*

Above right: *Cream jug in Cypher pattern by Portmeirion, 1963.*

Right: *Cream jug and sugar bowl in Jupiter pattern by Portmeirion, 1963. Difficulties with the glaze composition meant that Jupiter remained in production for a very short period.*

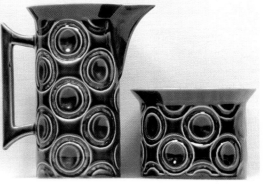

and Stylecraft shapes.

The multi-faceted nature of 1960s fashion is illustrated by the variety of patterns adorning the Fine shape. Although Fine was very successful, managing the huge range of patterns proved problematic for the company. The difficulties involved in catching the 'fashion mood' were brought into sharp perspective during the second half of the decade with the company's attempts at shape design. More risky than pattern design because of the higher development costs involved, shapes like MQ2 (1966) and Portobello (1967), inspired by studio pottery, were not very successful and proved

Patio on Fashion shape by Jessie Tait for W. R. Midwinter, c.1959–60. This pattern is typical of the transitional types that lasted well into the new decade.

Above left: *Aztec on Studio shape by Alan Rogers for J. & G. Meakin, 1965.*

Above right: *Cadiz on Studio shape by Alan Rogers for J. & G. Meakin, 1967.*

financially damaging to the company.

These pressures partly explain the reasons behind the takeover of Midwinter by **J. & G. Meakin** in 1968. This was ironic in that Meakin's had established its financial success during the 1960s on the Studio shape (1964), which owed much to the example of Fine. Like Fine, Studio was successful because it was a vehicle for a wide range of surface pattern designs reflecting the shifting 1960s tastes. These ranged from the stolidly traditional to pure Psychedelia. The success of Studio was due to its ability to act as the basis for a compromise between these two extremes, thus capturing the greatest possible share of the market. An example of this is Topic (1967) by Alan Rogers, which according to *The Pottery Gazette* '... brought a graphic and modern approach to bear on the basic theme of the English countryside ... thus producing a marriage between flora and Carnaby Street'.

Topic on Studio shape by Alan Rogers for J. & G. Meakin, 1967.

Black basalt coffee ware by Robert Minkin for Wedgwood, c.1964.

That J. & G. Meakin were themselves taken over by **Wedgwood** in 1970 indicates the pressures of the fashion cycle on companies in the medium-price sector of the market. It demonstrates that established fine china firms were also feeling the need to redefine themselves, entering new sectors of the market. For Wedgwood this need had arisen during the early 1960s. They took a new design-led approach with the Design 63 range, which included a new use of black basalt, a traditional Wedgwood body, and sets designed to be sold 'off the shelf' in cartons, such as Bermuda, '... designed particularly for young couples'. The company also embraced the enthusiasm for oven-to-table ware with shapes such as Pennine (1965) and Blue Pacific (1969).

Left: *Bermuda pattern on Bohemia shape by Robert Minkin for Wedgwood, 1963.*

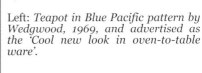

Above: *Examples of Pennine oven-to-table ware by Wedgwood, 1965.*

Left: *Teapot in Blue Pacific pattern by Wedgwood, 1969, and advertised as the 'Cool new look in oven-to-table ware'.*

21

Teacup and saucer in Pacifico on Sussex shape by Spode, 1965. Based on native North American symbols, the pattern was, according to 'The Pottery Gazette' (1965), '... all set for top favour with the young moderns'.

Other fine china companies also felt these forces. **Spode**, buoyed up by the success of the modern Royal College shape during the late 1950s, introduced the stoneware Sussex shape in 1965. Bearing what was described as '... a distinct family resemblance' to Royal College, it was modern enough to be accepted for the Council of Industrial Design's Design Index.

For **Royal Doulton** the adaptation to new trends was rather more measured with the introduction in 1966 of Tempo, a new shape in English translucent. Patterns developed for the shape, including Morning Star of the same year, had antecedents in 1950s patterns like Desert Star (1955). It was left to subsidiary companies like Ridgway to cater wholeheartedly for the demand for oven-to-table ware through shapes such as Phase One (1970).

Smaller firms in Staffordshire reacted cautiously to the stylistic trends of the 1960s. **British Anchor** employed consultant designers to produce the Rutland (1963), Impact (1966) and

Left: *Part coffee set in Impact shape designed by Tom Arnold for British Anchor, 1966.*

Right: *Cup and saucer in Taurus the Bull pattern on Sandon shape by Palissy, 1967. Advertised as '... a new version on a theme whose origin is lost in antiquity', the inappropriate flower motif on the saucer was removed in later versions.*

Small dish in Contessa pattern on Sandon shape by Palissy, 1967, and described as 'An interpretation from old tapestries'.

Strata (1967) shapes, which were modern and also able to carry decoration of the traditional variety. Firms like **Palissy** relied heavily on pattern design to cope with changing fashions.

Many smaller firms in the Potteries struggled to keep pace with the fickle demands of consumers. As a result, the 1960s were a period of large-scale amalgamation and takeover. Some design-conscious firms of the previous decade disappeared as independent companies. These included **John Beswick** (taken over by Doulton in 1969), the partnership between **Susie Cooper** and **R. H. & S. L. Plant** (taken over by Wedgwood in 1966), and **Aynsley** (taken over by Waterford Glass in 1970). Companies like **Staffordshire Potteries** prospered in the new atmosphere. A new design team with the latest high-capacity kiln equipment ensured that the company produced designs that were consistently in tune with the vagaries of fashion during the 1960s.

The success of the 'outpotters' (manufacturers outside the Stoke-on-Trent area) was built on solid foundations established during

Left: *Cup and saucer in Zorba pattern by Beswick, 1969.*

Ware from the Crescendo range in '... bright and fashionable colours' by Enoch Wedgwood (Tunstall) Ltd, 1968.

A selection of Staffordshire Potteries' Barbecue Beakers, 1968.

the previous decade. The lead in design was taken up during the 1960s by the Dorset firm of **Poole**. The company already had a reputation for good design based on modernist principles. During the 1950s its design policy was to consolidate this reputation through a limited range of well-established shapes decorated in conservative colours. By the early 1960s the trade press was suggesting that these might be too plain for modern tastes. This helps to explain the radical changes to design policy at the company steered by Robert Jefferson, a designer who had trained at the Royal College of Art, with experience of the Staffordshire pottery industry.

Jefferson's contribution can be seen through two strikingly different ranges. The Lucullus range of oven-to-table ware (1962) combined a contemporary development of the soft organic shapes for which Poole was famed with an approach to decoration that came from his experience of

Tray in an olive-green glaze from the Poole Studio Spring Collection, 1964.

Above: *A representative range of Studio shapes designed by Robert Jefferson for Poole, 1961–3.*

Below: *Dishes designed and painted by Robert Jefferson for Poole, 1962–4.*

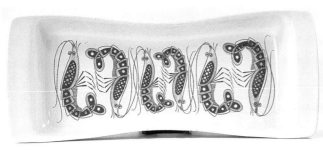

Serving dish from the Lucullus oven-to-table ware collection, launched by Poole in 1962.

Sea Crest and Blue Lace designed by Tony Morris and Guy Sydenham for Poole, 1967–8.

modern printing technology in Staffordshire. *Design* magazine (1961) described the outcome as a 'Paradigm in Pottery'.

The Delphis range was more radical and was launched commercially after a couple of years of research by Jefferson together with Guy Sydenham and Tony Morris. It was a novel combination of craft aesthetics, utilising hand-thrown forms and textures incised into the surface of the still wet clay, with bright, modern colours from commercially available glazes. Patterns were usually abstract and captured the developing interest in Psychedelia while retaining an individual quality. Critics were impressed by the combination of modern production facilities with an approach to design paralleling that in Scandinavia, where designers were encouraged to work as freely and imaginatively as possible. Delphis was intended for limited production, but the range epitomised Poole's independence

An advertising photograph for Poole's Delphis range, 1966.

An advertising photograph for Poole's Delphis range, 1966.

from the constraints of tradition felt by Staffordshire manufacturers, becoming a mainstay of production during the 1960s and 1970s.

Like Poole, **Hornsea**'s approach during the early 1960s was built upon established success. Hornsea had gained a firm reputation for design innovation during the late 1950s. Many of the successful shapes and patterns continued into the 1960s. The Fauna range continued to be made, but Hornsea's modern production during the early 1960s was based on elaborations of fluted and ribbed forms decorated with inlaid colour. Ranges such as the very successful Rainbow (1961) made concessions to growing demand for bright, abstract colour, whilst the geometric forms of Home Décor (from 1959) echoed the qualities of The Look. Hornsea's concern with a high standard of design led to a large proportion of the factory's products being included in the

Below: *Salt and pepper in the hugely successful Rainbow range. Hornsea, 1961.*

Below: *Vases in the Home Décor range modelled by John Clappison for Hornsea and in production 1959–62.*

27

Hornsea Studiocraft vases, 1966, which in their geometric decoration embody The Look.

COID's Design Index.

The greatest marketing success during the 1960s for Hornsea, and one that identifies the company as a technological innovator, was Heirloom (1967), together with its later derivatives, Saffron and Brontë. This was Hornsea's first complete tableware range. It used a novel glaze-resist technique to achieve its distinctive geometric pattern, alternating glazed and unglazed surfaces to dramatic effect. Available in three colours (Lakeland Green, Autumn Brown and Midnight Blue), the range was so successful at home and abroad that most of the company's production capacity was given over to it during the last years of the decade.

Poole and Hornsea were clearly significant forces in British ceramic manufacture during the 1960s, but the achievement of smaller outpotter firms working on the dividing line between industry and craft pottery should not be underestimated either.

Above: *Storage jars in (left to right) Brontë, Heirloom and Saffron patterns. Hornsea, late 1960s.*

Left: *Detail of Hornsea's Heirloom pattern demonstrating the decorative effect achieved through innovative use of the silkscreen-printing process.*

Stacking saucer, beaker and plate in Mad Hatter pattern by the Honiton Pottery, 1968.

These included the **Rye Pottery**, which celebrated its centenary in 1969 and was noted for producing pieces that were modern, yet with a handcrafted quality. Another firm, the **Honiton Pottery**, illustrates that small manufacturers often adapted more quickly to 1960s fashion than the larger Staffordshire firms, with its bright, modern patterns like the 'Carnabyesque' range Mad Hatter (1968). Equally, small firms like the **Haverfordwest Pottery** were included in the Design Index, earning the Design Centre 'kitemark' badge for their ranges. This is an indication of not only the success of craft-oriented potteries in producing good modern design but also the shifts within the British design establishment of the 1960s.

Part coffee service from the Holkham Pottery, a small concern notable for its employment of innovative designers, 1960s.

29

— Designers as professionals —

The significance of the designer as a key member of the management team had been established during the 1950s. It was during the 1960s that the designer became involved in all stages of the production process, from manufacturing to consumption.

Nowhere is this better shown than in the career of **Terence Conran**, who during the 1950s had played an important role in establishing Midwinter as a company recognised for its designs. In 1964 he founded Habitat, selling products in an environment conducive to the youthful consumers who were such a powerful force in the 1960s high street. The success of Habitat and other firms ensured that design remained a fundamental concern of management throughout the decade.

The changing retailing environment meant that the role of the designer changed too. At Wedgwood in-house teams worked alongside consultant designers and also with designers from companies that had been acquired or merged with Wedgwood such as **Susie Cooper**.

By the late 1950s Susie Cooper was turning away from the earthenware designs with which she had succeeded during the inter-war period and towards designs for bone china. This change was linked to a merger with R. H. & S. L. Plant Ltd in 1958 as Tuscan Holdings. The new alliance allowed Cooper to retain her independence as a designer and build on the success of her Can shape (1958). Can made reference to eighteenth-century shapes,

Above: *Nordic shape for Tuscan China by Richard Brockman, mid 1960s.*

Right: *Saucer in the Keystone pattern on Can shape by Susie Cooper for Wedgwood, 1968.*

and its severe, straight-sided form became the vehicle for dozens of Susie Cooper and later (1966 onwards) Wedgwood patterns. Can was suited to representing The Look of the early 1960s in ceramics, but Cooper's early designs for the shape are transitional rather than revolutionary. Patterns such as Dresden Spray and Black Fruit (1958) are reminiscent of the hand decoration, lithographic and aerographic techniques that had underpinned her success in the past.

Although Susie Cooper demonstrated her ability to tap into fashion trends with patterns such as Art Nouveau (1965), it was only when the company was taken over by the Wedgwood Group that transition to the needs of the contemporary style occurred in her work. This appears in a series of patterns for the Can shape, including Carnaby Daisy, Heraldry (c.1968) and Diabolo (1968), that made use of the Covercoat transfer process, which produced a bold, striking use of colour to distinctly modern effect. Susie Cooper's work proved a continuing success throughout the 1960s in terms of both sales and official recognition. By 1971 eighteen of her patterns on her Can shape were featured in the Design Index.

In contrast to Susie Cooper, **Jessie Tait** was an in-house designer with Midwinter who remained a company employee

Left: *Teapot in the Diabolo pattern on Can shape by Susie Cooper for Wedgwood, 1968.*

Below left: *Roulette by Kathy Winkle for James Broadhurst & Sons, late 1960s. Winkle designed for Broadhurst throughout the 1950s and 1960s, but it was only from the mid 1960s onwards that her name started to be used on backstamps. Today her designs are becoming increasingly collectable.*

Below right: *Coffee can and saucer in the Carnaby Daisy pattern on Can shape by Susie Cooper for Wedgwood, 1968.*

A range of patterns on Midwinter's revised Fine shape. Left to right: Madeira by Jessie Tait, Broadway, and Spanish Garden by Jessie Tait, all 1960s.

throughout her career, and yet who managed to build a substantial reputation for her work from the 1950s onwards. By the early 1960s this reputation was strengthened further by the way Tait adapted to the demands of the new fashions.

This adaptability is shown through the patterns she designed for the Fine shape, ranging from the hand-painted Mexicana (1966) to the hugely successful lithographic transfer pattern Spanish Garden (1966), which remained in production for around two decades. Spanish Garden demonstrated the interest in stylised floral patterns related to the Art Nouveau revival, which in turn was to lead on to the Psychedelia of the early 1970s, although it was conservative enough to appeal to many people. It was also the first pattern to be introduced on the revised Fine shape and its success confirmed Tait's versatility as a designer, acting as the catalyst for a range of related patterns by her, such as Country Garden (1968).

Jessie Tait worked closely at Midwinter with **David Queensberry**, described by *The Pottery Gazette* (1962) as 'the unquestioned leader' of 'the whole modern movement in domestic ceramics'. Queensberry is the best-known of a group of design consultants who were trained as ceramic designers, but who were not tied to any one firm. During the

David Queensberry (left) and Roy Midwinter working on the MQ2 shape, 1967.

32

Roulette by Tom Arnold for Gibson & Sons, 1964. Contemporary advertising suggested that it combined 'the quality and richness of the eighteenth century with modern line and sophistication'.

1950s the design consultant began to be a significant force in the pottery industry and contributed to the acceptance of the designer as a professional. This process was speeded up during the early 1960s in the art schools when the technically oriented National Diploma in Design (NDD) was phased out, and the Diploma in Art and Design (DipAD), which had degree status, was introduced. Queensberry played a full part in this process, having been appointed professor of ceramics at the Royal College of Art in 1959.

A core group of consultant designers was formed during the 1960s. Of these, **Tom Arnold**, who also trained at the Royal College of Art, stands out for the versatility and abundance of his design work, which brings a contemporary feel to the products of a wide range of manufacturers whilst managing to retain their individual design identities. Arnold suggested in a lecture (1964) that 'It is essential to move slowly; if buyers and retailers are used to a certain character coming from a firm, then the image must not be broken suddenly.' This philosophical and pragmatic approach was demonstrated in a range of products including: the Caldor shape for Empire; Rutland (1962) and Gayday (1963) for T. G. Green; the Atlanta shape for Wood & Sons (1965); and the

Cerix shape by Tom Arnold with pattern by Alan Swale for Empire Porcelain, 1961. This was the first Empire design to be included in the Design Index.

Shape produced in 1962 by Robert Welch for A. T. Finney & Company (Duchess Bone China).

Impact (1966) and Strata (1967) shapes for British Anchor. Most startling are Arnold's designs for Gibson & Sons. These include the traditionally inspired Roulette (1964) in 'red body ware', with its use of impressed decoration echoing Gillian Pemberton's work for Denby with Chevron, and the dramatic Starburst (1964), which made use of modern, utilitarian shapes and screen-printed decoration.

The 1960s were a decade when there was a steady shift away from the specialist ceramic designer. An editorial in *Tableware* (1964) worried that 'There is a danger ... that the specialist pottery designer may become a much rarer bird. The big general design names will tend to assume the limelight, the pottery designer remaining in the factory refining shapes and decorations.' One of the designers who prompted this concern was Robert Welch, a Royal College graduate who made his name as a designer of metalwork and cutlery but also designed ceramic tableware. His first work, in 1962, for A. T. Finney & Company (Duchess Bone China) was a shape which attracted much press interest. Its clean, modern lines appealed to the industry and to the Council of Industrial Design, which had already given Welch a Duke of Edinburgh's Award for Elegant Design for his work in metal.

Alongside the work of Robert Welch can be placed that of **Gerald Benney**, a silversmith who became known in the late 1950s for pieces in silver which in their long, attenuated forms and textured surfaces paralleled trends being taken up by the pottery industry. His work in ceramics is more limited than that of Welch, but designs such as Ondine (1965) on his Albion shape for Ridgway Potteries show a continuing interest in the relationship between form and surface decoration.

Ondine on Albion shape by Gerald Benney for Ridgway Potteries, 1965.

Above left: *Soup dish and plate in Focus on Fine shape by Barbara Brown for W. R. Midwinter, 1964.*

Above right: *Cup and saucer in Kismet pattern on Fine shape by Joti Bhowmik for W. R. Midwinter, 1968.*

Left: *Cup and saucer in Bengal pattern on Fine shape by Joti Bhowmik for W. R. Midwinter, 1968.*

It was in design for fashion and textiles that The Look of the early 1960s was most forcefully felt. Not surprisingly pottery manufacturers wished to follow this trend. Particularly significant in this context is the employment by Midwinter of two textile designers, **Barbara Brown** and **Joti Bhowmik**, each bringing the aesthetics of textiles to bear upon the Fine shape in different ways. In Brown's case this was represented by Focus (1964), a best-selling pattern that in its severe, geometric qualities both harmonised with Fine and perfectly summed up The Look. Bhowmik's patterns Kismet and Bengal (1968) were far more overtly textile in origin but, as Bhowmik was anxious to emphasise, 'I work with the shape first'. Demonstrating what David Queensberry described as a 'fantastic sense of colour', Kismet and Bengal are unusual examples of two colourways utilising the same basic design.

Fleur pattern by Berit Ternel for T. G. Green, 1961.

The part that designers played for the outpotters was, if anything, more significant. Unlike the expanding industrial combines of Stoke-on-Trent, these businesses were too small to be able to afford 'star' names. The exceptions included the flower bricks produced by the Bristol Pottery to the designs of the internationally renowned designer **Lucienne Day**, and the continuing work by the textile designer **Berit Ternel** for T. G. Green, including Fleur (1961).

Small and medium-sized firms such as Hornsea and Poole kept up by employing young innovative designers, often from the wave of new talent graduating from the Royal College of Art from the late 1950s onwards. Hornsea employed **John Clappison** in

Ceramic Textile Screen designed by John Clappison for Hornsea and exhibited at the Tea Centre, London, in November 1966.

Tray in an olive-green glaze from the Poole Studio Spring Collection, 1964.

1958 and his influence was twofold. First, he focused the company on issues of quality in design, drawing on the values promoted by the COID. Secondly, he showed through his technical understanding (particularly of screen-print decoration processes) that successful products came about most often from a holistic approach to design issues.

Robert Jefferson's role at Poole was somewhat different. Although he also trained at the Royal College of Art, he came

An advertising photograph for Poole's Delphis range, 1967.

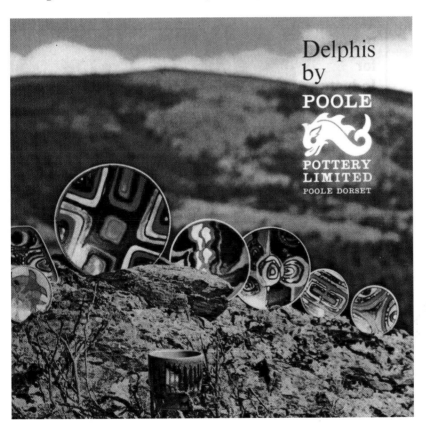

Delphis
by
POOLE
POTTERY
LIMITED
POOLE DORSET

Patrician by Gillian Pemberton for Langley Pottery, the catering and hotel ware division of Denby, 1963.

from an older generation, joining the company with substantial experience of the industrial climate in Stoke-on-Trent. From this, he recognised that design policy within the company should concentrate upon establishing an aesthetic that was clearly different from the products of North Staffordshire.

Similarly influential was the contribution that **Gillian Pemberton** made to the success of Denby during the 1960s. Leaving the Royal College of Art in 1960 she immediately joined the company. She worked initially at its catering and hotel ware division, Langley Pottery, most notably revamping the Patrician range (1963). Her greatest contribution, however, was her ability to harmonise with the stylistic trends of the decade, whether in the rather severe and geometric Chevron or the more freely designed Arabesque (1963), whilst at the same time keeping within the design policies of the company.

Teapot in Arabesque by Gillian Pemberton for Denby, 1963.

Further reading

Baynton, V., May, H., and Morton, J. *The Beswick Collector's Handbook*. Kevin Francis, 1986.

Dex, L. *Hornsea Pottery: A Collector's Guide, 1947–1967*. Beck Books, 1989.

Eatwell, A. *Susie Cooper Productions*. Victoria and Albert Museum, 1987.

Hannah, F. *Ceramics: Twentieth Century Design*. Bell & Hyman, 1986.

Hawkins, J. *The Poole Potteries*. Barrie & Jenkins, 1980.

Hayward, L. *Poole Pottery: Carter & Company and Their Successors 1873–1995*. Richard Dennis, 1995.

Hopwood, I. and G. *Denby Pottery 1809–1997: Dynasties and Designers*. Richard Dennis, 1997.

Jackson, L. *The Sixties: Decade of Design Revolution*. Phaidon, 1998.

Jenkins, S. *Midwinter Pottery: A Revolution in British Tableware*. Richard Dennis, 1997.

Jenkins, S., and McKay, S. P. *Portmeirion Pottery*. Richard Dennis, 2000.

Niblett, K. *Dynamic Design: The British Pottery Industry 1940–1980*. Stoke-on-Trent City Museum and Art Gallery, 1990.

Opie, J. *Scandinavia: Ceramics and Glass in the Twentieth Century*. Victoria and Albert Museum, 1989.

Peat, Alan. *Midwinter: A Collector's Guide*. Cameron & Hollis, 1992.

Stanton, V., and Cooper-Willis, E. *The Story of Portmeirion Potteries*. Portmeirion Potteries, 1995.

Walker, S. *Queensberry Hunt: Creativity and Industry*. Fourth Estate, 1992.

Watson, O. *British Studio Pottery*. Phaidon, 1990.

Woodhouse, A. *Susie Cooper*. Trilby, 1992.

David Puxley with examples of his work in black basalt stoneware for Wedgwood, early 1960s.

Places to visit

Brighton Museum and Art Gallery, Church Street, Brighton, East Sussex BN1 1UE. Telephone: 01273 290900. (Closed for redevelopment until 2001.)

Bristol City Museum and Art Gallery, Queen's Road, Bristol BS8 1RL. Telephone: 0117 922 3571. Website: www.bristol-city.gov.uk

British Museum, Great Russell Street, London WC1B 3DG. Telephone: 020 7636 1555. Website: www.britishmuseum.co.uk

Design Museum, 28 Shad Thames, London SE1 2YD. Telephone: 020 7403 6933. Website: www.designmuseum.org

Geffrye Museum, Kingsland Road, London E2 8EA. Telephone: 020 7739 9893. Website: www.geffrye-museum.org.uk

Hornsea Museum, 11 Newbegin, Hornsea, East Yorkshire HU18 1AB. Telephone: 01964 533443.

Manchester City Art Galleries, Mosley Street, Manchester M2 3JL. Telephone: 0161 236 5244. Website: www.u-net.com/set/mcag/cag.html (Closed for redevelopment until 2001.)

Potteries Museum and Art Gallery, Bethesda Street, Hanley, Stoke-on-Trent, Staffordshire ST1 3DE. Telephone: 01782 232323. Website: www.stoke.gov.uk/museums

Royal Museum of Scotland, Chambers Street, Edinburgh EH1 1JF. Telephone: 0131 225 7534. Website: www.nms.ac.uk

Victoria and Albert Museum, Cromwell Road, South Kensington, London SW7 2RL. Telephone: 020 7942 2000. Website: www.vam.ac.uk

Tropic pattern on Eclipse shape by Tom Arnold for H. Aynsley & Company Ltd, 1968.